1M followers

I am lovable

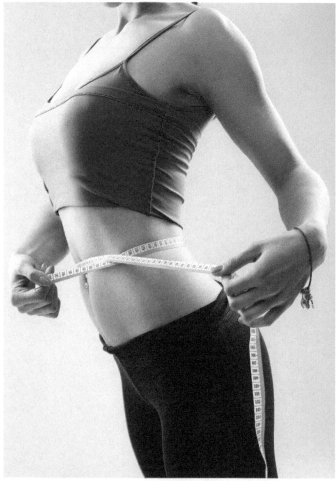

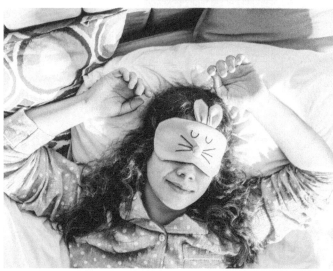

YOU ARE ENOUGH

FLAWED AND still WORTHY

EVERY BODY IS BEAUTIFUL

I'M PRETTY

I'M BEAUTIFUL

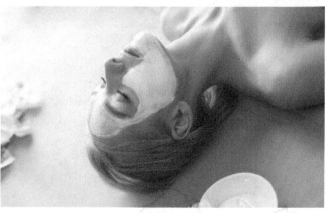

STAY HEALTHY

I'M FINALLY CLEAN

TAKE RISKS

GO WITH THE FLOW

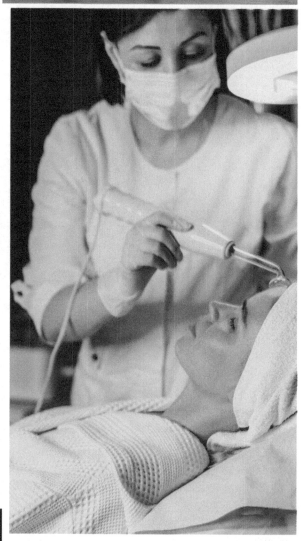

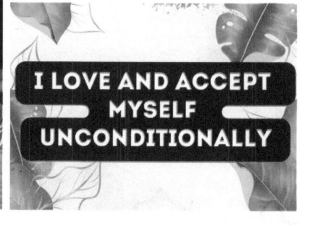

I LOVE AND ACCEPT
MYSELF
UNCONDITIONALLY

YOUR

Wave is

WAITING

GOOD VIBES

ENJOY EVERY MOMENT

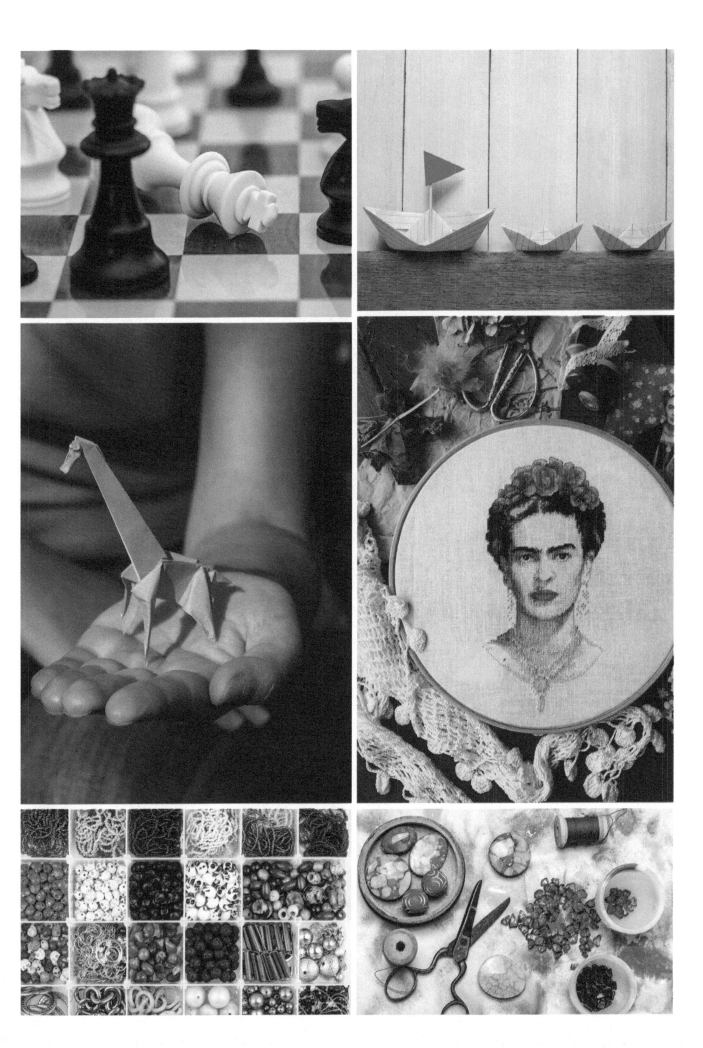

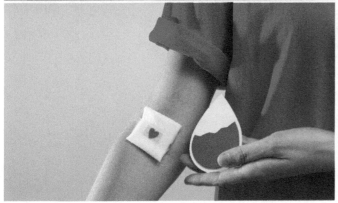

I attract wealth and abundance into my life with ease

Poster For Your Bedroom

YOUR NAME
Your Address Place
Tel: 99999-0000

000123

DATE

PAY TO THE
ORDER OF _____

$

_____ DOLLARS 🔒

◆ **NAME BANK**
Bank Address Place
BANK Tel: 888-9999

RE _____

AUTHORIZED SIGNATURE _____

123456789   123456789   001234

YOUR NAME
Your Address Place
Tel: 99999-0000

000123

DATE

PAY TO THE
ORDER OF _____

$

_____ DOLLARS 🔒

◆ **NAME BANK**
Bank Address Place
BANK Tel: 888-9999

RE _____

AUTHORIZED SIGNATURE _____

123456789   123456789   001234

YOUR NAME
Your Address Place
Tel: 99999-0000

000123

DATE

PAY TO THE
ORDER OF _____

$

_____ DOLLARS 🔒

◆ **NAME BANK**
Bank Address Place
BANK Tel: 888-9999

RE _____

AUTHORIZED SIGNATURE _____

123456789   123456789   001234

YOUR NAME
Your Address Place
Tel: 99999-0000

000123

DATE

PAY TO THE
ORDER OF _____

$

_____ DOLLARS 🔒

◆ **NAME BANK**
Bank Address Place
BANK Tel: 888-9999

RE _____

AUTHORIZED SIGNATURE _____

123456789   123456789   001234

0 0 0 0 0 0 0 0 0 0 0

1 1 1 1 1 1 1 1 1 1 1

2 2 2 2 2 2 2 2 2 2 2

3 3 3 3 3 3 3 3 3 3

4 4 4 4 4 4 4 4 4 4 4

5 5 5 5 5 5 5 5 5 5 5

6 6 6 6 6 6 6 6 6 6 6

7 7 7 7 7 7 7 7 7 7 7

8 8 8 8 8 8 8 8 8 8 8

9 9 9 9 9 9 9 9 9 9 9

$ $ $ $ $ $ $ $

$ $ $ $ $ $ $ $

€ € € € € € €

€ € € € € € €

C$ C$ C$ C$ C$ C$ C$

C$ C$ C$ C$ C$ C$ C$

£ £ £ £ £ £ £

£ £ £ £ £ £ £

Don't Over-Think It

MAKE today MAGICAL

I CAN DO IT

STAY COMMITTED

DREAM PLAN DO!

NEVER STOP

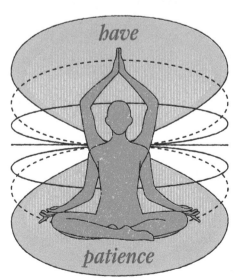

have

patience

You're a STAR

Never Give Up

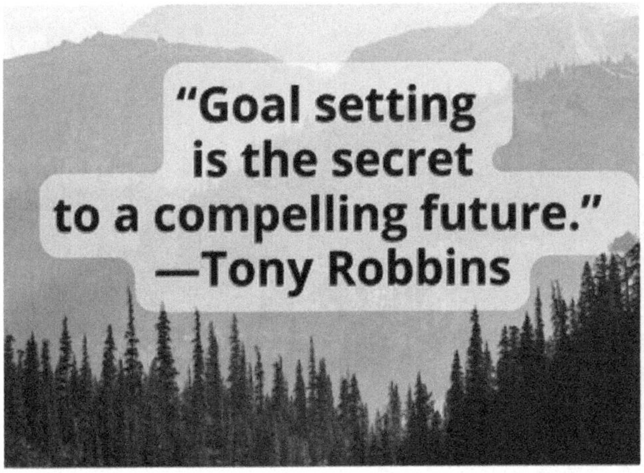

"Goal setting
is the secret
to a compelling future."
—Tony Robbins

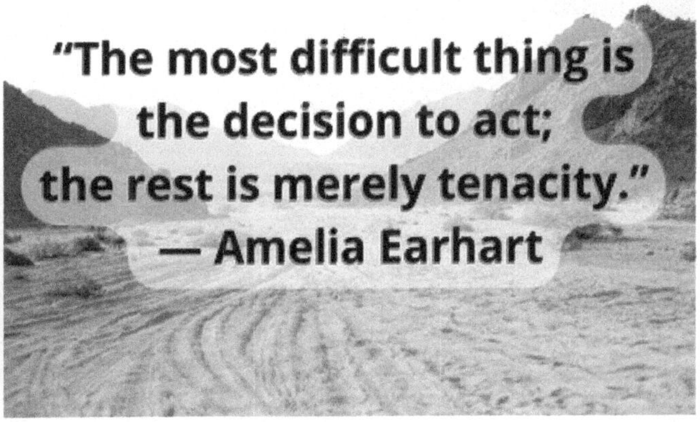

"The most difficult thing is
the decision to act;
the rest is merely tenacity."
— Amelia Earhart

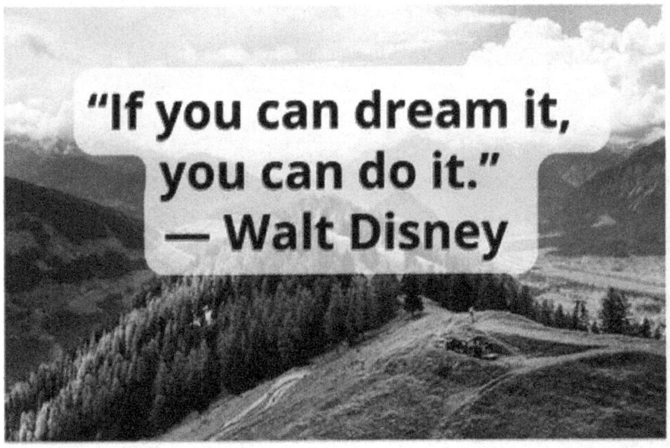

"If you can dream it,
you can do it."
— Walt Disney

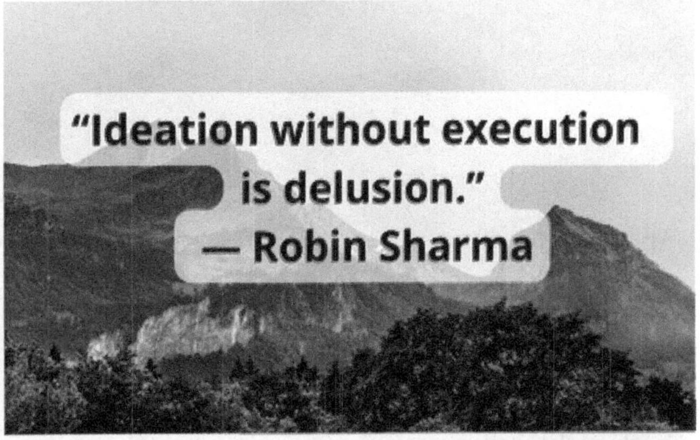

"Ideation without execution
is delusion."
— Robin Sharma

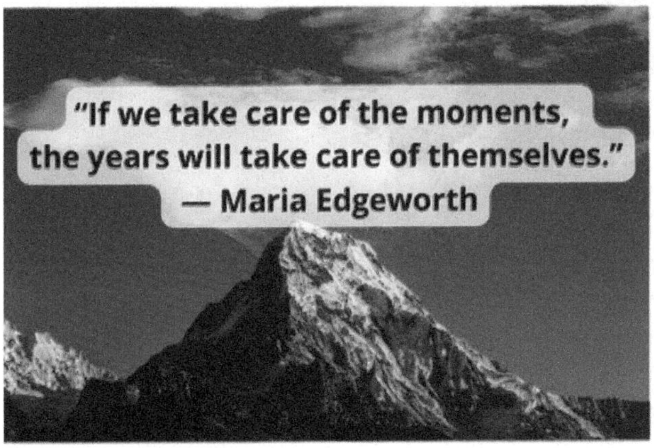

"If we take care of the moments,
the years will take care of themselves."
— Maria Edgeworth

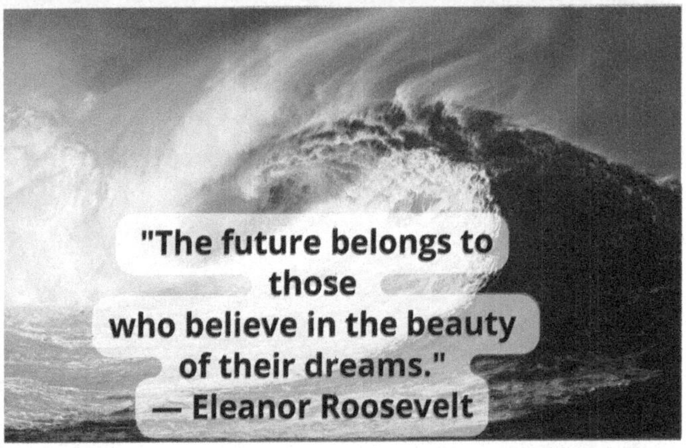

"The future belongs to
those
who believe in the beauty
of their dreams."
— Eleanor Roosevelt

"The longer I live,
the more beautiful life becomes."
– Frank Lloyd Wright

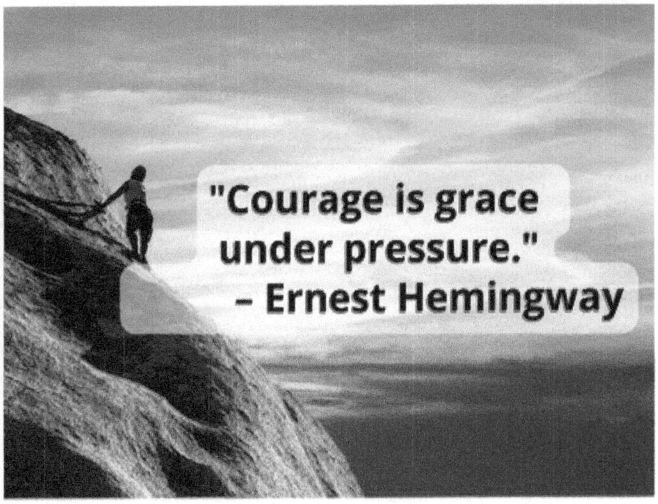

"Courage is grace
under pressure."
– Ernest Hemingway

How to create a vision board that is perfect for you?

Dear You,
Welcome to the Vision Board Clip Art Book for Women — a roadmap to your dreams and aspirations! Congratulations on seizing the driver's seat in your life transformation journey. By embracing the power of vision, you're embarking on a journey of self-discovery and empowerment that will shape your future in remarkable ways. Let's embark on this transformative journey together, starting with the foundational steps to create your vision board.

Set yourself for success

Gather your materials: Poster board or corkboard, printed images from this book, and your photos, scissors, glue, markers, and any other decorative elements that speak to you.

Reflection: Before diving into the visual realm, take a moment to reflect on your desires and aspirations. Ask yourself probing questions:

- What brings me joy and fulfillment in life?
- What are my deepest dreams and aspirations?
- Where do I see myself in the next year or a decade from now?
- Who and What Surrounds Me?
- What Does My Lifestyle Look Like?
- How Do I Create Value for the World?
- What Am I Known For?
- What Do My Key Relationships Feel Like?

BELIEVE
YOU CAN

Dream it, see it, achieve it: create your vision board

Gather your materials and reflect on what truly excites you. Pick images and words that resonate with your aspirations. No wrong choices here - get creative! Arrange them to tell your story, the story of your ambitions coming true. Feel the power surge as your vision takes shape!

Download 3 presents by scanning this QR-code

- Worksheets with reflection questions.
- Tips for creating a visually stunning vision board.
- **The extended digital version of this vision board book is twice the size of the original.**

P.S. *In case you failed to scan QR code email us with access request to* **kdpbookssuccess@gmail.com**

Made in the USA
Las Vegas, NV
17 October 2024